Music From the Heart

Original Songs for Mountain Dulcimer

with instruction for chord-melody style

Tom McConnell

With Audio Web Companion
Containing samples of songs available at:

http://www.musicbytmcc.com/heartsongs

AIRWAY PUBLISHING

AIRWAY PUBLISHING

Music From the Heart
Original Songs for Mountain Dulcimer

Tom McConnell

Airway Publishing
Muncie, Indiana, USA

All songs composed and written by Tom McConnell
Tablatures produced using Tabledit™
Instructional graphics by Tom McConnell
Cover art and photography by Mike McConnell

Printed by CreateSpace

McConnell, Tom   2015
Music from the heart: Original songs for mountain dulcimer
Muncie, IN: Airway Publishing

ISBN-10: 0986336904
ISBN-13: 978-0-9863369-0-4
http://www.musicbytmcc.com/heartsongs

42p

Table of Contents

Preface iv

INSTRUCTION: The Tablature 2

INSTRUCTION: Primer on Chord Shapes 3

INSTRUCTION: "*Yes I Do*" and "*Butterfly Waltz*" 6

Yes I Do 7

Butterfly Waltz 8

INSTRUCTION: Hammer-ons and Pull-offs 11

Back to the Glenns 12

Expressions 14

The Change Will Do Me Good 16

How I Try 18

Wishing for Wings 20

Just One More Song (A Song for Michael) 22

Scotty Smiles 24

The Break of Spring 26

When I Was A Boy 28

After All That We've Been Through 30

INSTRUCTION: Capo, Flat-Picking and Chopping 32

Letters from Andersonville 33

Seasons Lost 34

Who's That Knocking On the Door? 36

About the Author 38

Preface

Like most of those who may buy this book, I am a dulcimer hobbyist. I do not play professionally, and I have a "day job" that is my number one source of income. So for me, this work is one of passion – I play and write and share my music only because I love it!

This book of dulcimer tabs is different from most others in your local music store. Rather than writing tabs for well-known songs, I chose to include only original compositions in this book. You likely did not know these tunes when you first picked up this book. In my opinion, this means it took a sense of adventure for you jump into these songs, and I appreciate your courage!

Because of how and why I write music, these songs are very personal. Several have back-stories that are likely only of importance to me or certain friends or family members. I thank these individuals for the inspiration that I think is essential to creating songs that connect with listeners on an emotional level.

A friend told me to "close my eyes and play from the heart" when I was getting ready to record an album in 2001, *Playing from the Heart.* Several of the songs in this book appeared on that album, and the title of this book reflects that connection. My hope is that you will play these songs from *your* heart, with an expressive style, just as many of my friends add to their playing. Make the song your own expression!

I wish to thank Maureen Sellers, a performer and teacher I met several years ago at some workshops hosted by the Northeast Indiana Folk Music and Instrument Gathering in Shipshewana, IN. She was the first to encourage me to publish these songs, and gave me tips on the process. It took years to finish grad school so I could find time for this endeavor, but I still remember her advice. I also need to thank NEIFMIG for being my first live audience for my songs. I also owe thanks to Folkcraft Instruments and the Black Swamp Jam they host for being a new audience and an encouraging group of friends. Thanks also go to Stephen Seifert for his Tabledit tutorials. Without them, I'd still be wrestling with my tabs.

And most of all…

Thank you for choosing to learn my songs! You've brought a piece of me into your home, and I sincerely hope you enjoy playing this music!

Tom J. McConnell

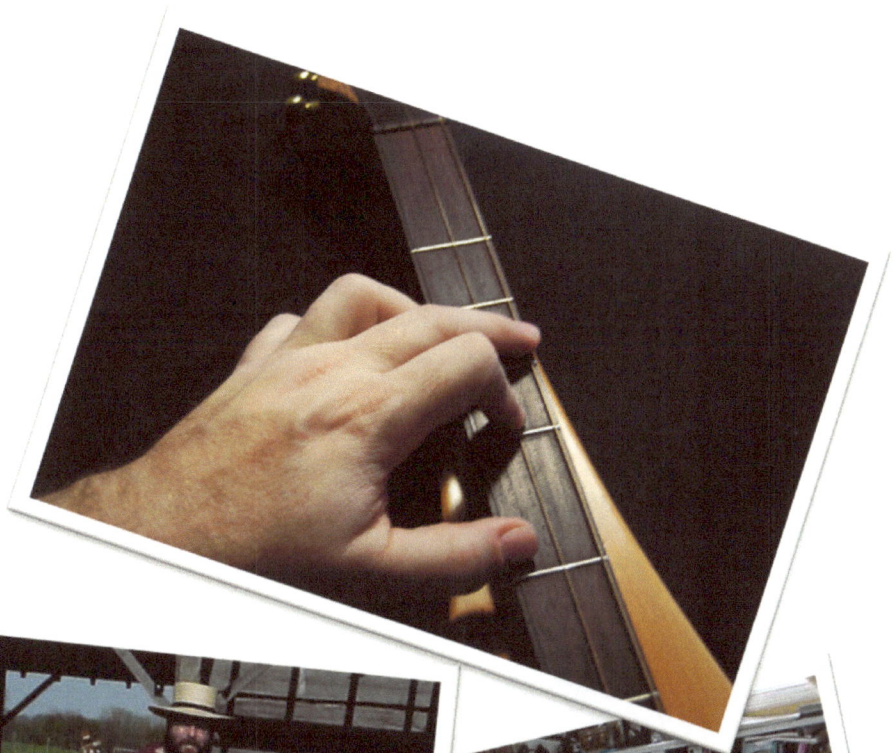

INSTRUCTION: The Tablature

The tabs in this book are presented in chord-melody style. That means you'll find the melody notes *and* chords. The melody will be played mostly on the "melody" string(s) on your dulcimer. Notation above the tabs will help with the rhythm of the notes, and for those who read music, you'll be able to "see" the tune or play it on another instrument.

But I also included chords with each bar. These chords can be played with other fingerings, so they are just my suggestions… and the way I play these songs. My playing style is to let the chords ring out, and to strum a steady pattern throughout the song.

FOR BEGINNERS: If you do not play chords, feel free to play the single-note melodies. One of the great things about the dulcimer is that drone sound of the instrument, and if you throw in a chord or two when needed, all the better.

All of the songs in this book are written in DAd', and any 1-5-8 tuning will work very well with these. I sometimes play these songs on a baritone in AEa', and I love that sound, especially with songs like *The Change Will Do Me Good* and *After All That We've Been Through.* You'll also find a pair of songs played with a capo, and one that is flat-picked. Watch for the text at the top of the page to cue you when a song is meant to be played in a different key or style.

I've also tossed in some instructions about chord shapes and fingerings that help facilitate chord-melody style, capos and arpeggios, and other helpful "instruction" as you go. By the way, some of those instructions may describe strum patterns. Just so you know… I'M AN OUTIE! That means my natural strum pattern use an out-stroke for the down-beat, with my hand moving away from my body. Some people are "innies" – they strum an in-stroke (toward their body). Either way works fine, but it may help you translate my instructions if you know that!

Samples of the Songs

Because these are not widely known songs, you may want to hear them as you learn and practice. My website has sample recordings to accompany this book. Most of the recordings are short, are a pace slow enough to let you follow along, and include only the dulcimer. A few are from my first CD, *Playing from the Heart,* a recording that includes samples of some of these songs. All the recordings are intended to help you learn the melody. You can find these samples at…

http://www.musicbytmcc.com/heartsongs/

INSTRUCTION: Primer on Chord Shapes

One of the best things about playing chords and chord-melody music is that you can fill in your music with rich harmonies that add something special to your playing. There are songs in which the drone of open bass and middle strings on a dulcimer is ideal – I'm not suggesting you always play full chords. But sometimes the sound of full chords just makes me smile!

The songs in this book are presented in a chord-melody style, mainly because that is what best conveyed my feelings when I wrote these songs. If you're not used to playing chords, this primer on chords may help. If, on the other hand, you'd rather just work on melodies, play the notes on the melody string (sometimes the middle string) and ignore the chord changes.

One of the challenges is learning "all those chords." The finger positions take some practice. Changing from one chord to another is even harder. Work at it! Pick a couple of chords that you find common in the music, and start strumming on one, then switch after a couple of measures. Switch back and forth for a while to build the muscle memory. It will become second nature! And in the meantime, here are some shortcuts.

Chord Shapes

Fortunately, chords on the dulcimer are far easier than on a guitar. You don't have to learn as many finger positions. If you learn a handful of basic "Chord Shapes," you'll be using chords in a short time! My first dulcimer teachers used the motto, "There are no notes on a dulcimer, just finger positions." I'll modify that now… "There is no need to learn many different chords on a dulcimer – just chord SHAPES!"

Chord shapes refer to patterns in the shapes you make if you "connect the dots" with the placement of your fingers on the frets. The shapes are very versatile – you can slide up (toward the bridge) or down (toward the tuning head) the fret board with the same shape, and you'll have different chords, or different voicing of the same chord. There are several different chord shapes, but most songs will have 3 or 4 that show up frequently. Other teaching books refer to these shapes, although I may include some names that differ from the others.

The diagrams on the next pages show the various shapes, and give some tab notation for examples of each. On my fret board diagram, I show three strings. If you play with a double melody string, remember that those two strings are tuned to the same note, so I will only talk about 3 strings (Bass, middle and melody).

The finger positions are my suggestions. You might choose a different combination of fingers for each chord, but I strongly suggest you try my diagrams. They leave my thumb free, allowing me to play melody lines while still holding chords. For the songs in this book, this is important – it is the "chord-melody" style you'll hear in the sample songs when you visit the website!

Chord Shapes

"Bar" chords – the correct term is "Barre," but I'm talking shapes, not correct music terms! These have all the strings held on the same fret. Some play by laying a finger across all three. I prefer to put my index, middle and ring fingers on the frets. Doing this lets me play melody notes by dropping a thumb or lifting a finger.

Examples			
1	3	4	5
1	3	4	5
1	3	4	5
Em	G	A	B

"Diagonal" chords – These form a diagonal line across the fret board. (This ain't rocket science!). These can be angled either up or down the fret board.

Examples			
2	4	3	5
3	3	4	6
4	2	5	7
D		Em	G

"L Shaped" chords – You guessed it! These make a letter "L." The melody string for this is played with the thumb, which lets you move that note up and down the string a bit. Very handy in chord-melody playing!

Examples			
1	2	3	4
1	2	3	4
3	4	5	6
Em	F#m	G	A

"Bracket" chords – This is *my* name for a chord in which you fret the bass and melody strings at the same fret, and leave the middle string open. I like to use my middle and ring fingers so my thumb and index fingers are ready to play melody notes!

Examples		
1	2	7
0	0	0
1	2	7
A	D	D

"Arrow Up" chords – The pattern created by these chords makes an triangle or an arrow. I call it an up arrow because it points UP the fretboard – Yes, that's up! As you move closer to the bridge, the notes get higher, so it MUST be up!

Examples		
1	2	5
2	3	6
1	2	5
A7	D	G

"Arrow Down" chords – If you read about the shapes for the Arrow Up chords, you can probably guess what these are… just turn the arrow so it points to the tuning head!

Examples		
2	3	6
1	2	5
2	3	6
Bm	D	C#m

"Stretch Diagonal" chords – These are diagonal chords in which one of the strings is played more than one fret up from the middle string. It requires a stretch, and some players with small hands don't like it, but give these a try. (You may want to use your middle and ring fingers instead of index and middle fingers.)

Examples			
1	4	3	6
2	2	4	4
4	1	6	3
A		C	

"Open Diagonal" chords – This is a two finger chord, and I used these often in my earlier songs. They fit the diagonal chord shape, but you simply leave the bass string open. When playing these chords, you can keep some of the drone effect that is typical of traditional dulcimer tunes, and still have the harmonies that come from chords.

Examples				
0	0	0	0	0
3	5	2	4	6
2	4	1	3	5
D	A		G	

INSTRUCTION: *"Yes I Do"* and *"Butterfly Waltz"*

The first two songs in this collection are both from *Playing from the Heart,* so they are among the earliest I've written. Both of these songs use very basic examples of the chords you'll need to play most songs on the dulcimer: D, A and G.

Strum Patterns
As you work on these songs, strum a basic waltz rhythm... "1, 2, 3-and", with an out-stroke on 1, 2 and 3, and an in-stroke on "-and." (Reverse those if you're an "innie!")

Common Moveable Chord Shapes
If you are not comfortable playing chords, these two songs are good opportunities to expand your techniques. As you're getting familiar with the song, try playing along with the entire song, but ONLY play the chord at the start of each measure. For instance, the first line of *"Yes I Do"* starts with a D chord (0-3-2), with the zero being the bass string!) Play that waltz strum pattern (1, 2, 3-and) for one measure, then switch to a different D chord (2-3-4) for one measure, and keep going! Don't try the melody notes just yet!

When you practice with these chords, try to use fingerings that do NOT include the thumb. Keep your "fret hand" (left hand for a right-handed player) relaxed and comfortable, and you'll quickly see how your thumb is in a great place to add melody notes. You should think about the chord SHAPES rather than the details – if you do this, you'll see that several of the chords in "Yes I Do" and "Butterfly Waltz" use the same shape. This makes these great songs to start with in this book.

TIPS

For the first D chord in measure 1 of *"Yes I Do"*, I put my index finger on the middle string at fret 3. My ring finger is on the melody string(s) – closest to your body- at fret 2. This leaves your thumb free to fret other notes as you slide the "open diagonal" shape up the fret board to other chords.

In "Butterfly Waltz," use this same shape in measures 1, 2, 7, 8, and most of the B section. Remember – keep your hand in the open diagonal, and use your thumb to play the melody notes between chords.

In measure 2 of "Yes I Do," play a D chord (2-3-4) – one of the diagonal chords. Use the fingering shown in the Primer. If your hand is relaxed, your ring finger should be perfectly positioned to fret the melody string on fret 2! Hold this down WHILE playing the 2-3-4 chord. The melody note on the 3rd beat can be played easily by just lifting your thumb – the ring finger is already there! This lets you switch from "diagonal" to "arrow down" with one small movement!

Yes I Do

by Tom McConnell
2015

Dulcimer tuning: DAd' (Mixolydian)

7

Butterfly Waltz

by Tom McConnell
2015

Dulcimer tuning: DAd' (Mixolydian)

DS al Fine

INSTRUCTION: Hammer-ons and Pull-offs
Tips for playing "*Back the Glenns*"

This song is another of my early compositions. The song has a very Celtic feel to it. My family's history took us from Scotland through a part of Ireland known as "the Glenns." The song's title reflects the historical reference. The chord structure in the song is pretty simple... D, A and G like many basic dulcimer tunes, and most of the chords are either "bracket" chords or "open diagonals" on the melody and middle strings.

> Listen to a sample of "*Back to the Glenns*" at http://www.musicbytmcc.com/heartsongs

But as you listen to the sample of this song, you should notice the hammer-ons and pull-offs that give the song it's lilting rhythm. You'll see these techniques used in several fiddle tunes that are popular among dulcimer jam groups.

The hammer-on technique is easier to learn than the pull-off, so let's start there! And you'll see a good place to practice a hammer-on in the first measure of the song. Try it slowly at first, and speed up when you're more comfortable with it later.

Hammer-on - In the first measure, the D chord is the easiest of all chords... all open strings! Strum all three strings ONCE, and without strumming again, place your ring finger on the 1st fret – and use some force with it! You're hammering onto the string, after all! If you hit the fretboard hard enough, it will ring through cleanly with an E note... and you still have not strummed again! Then lift your finger and strum the open D chord again.

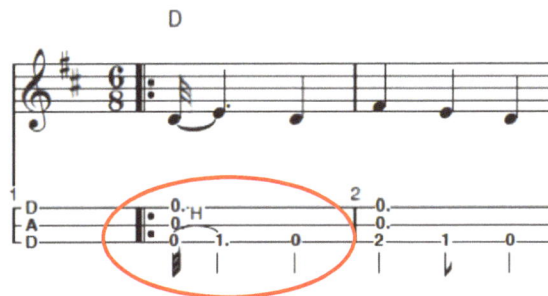

Pull-off – The pull-off takes a bit more practice, but stick with it. It adds a lot to your playing! With the pull-off, you'll always start with a finger on one of the frets. In this song, measure 30 is a good example. This starts with a D chord (0-0-2). But instead of playing it with one finger, I use two – my index on the 2nd fret, melody string, and my ring or middle finger on the first fret. Then just pull the finger off, but *toward your body!* This actually plucks the string, to let the note ring through! In this example, you then lift your hand, and strum the open D chord.

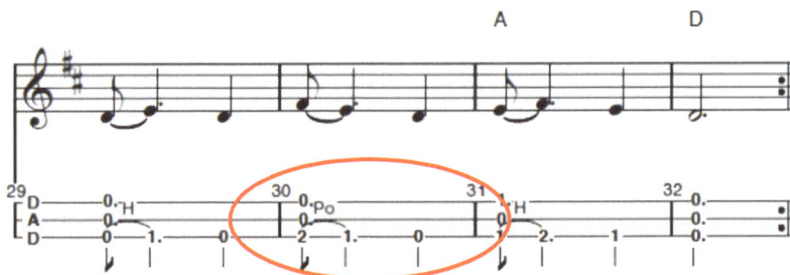

Back to the Glenns

by Tom McConnell
2015

Dulcimer tuning: DAd' (Mixolydian)

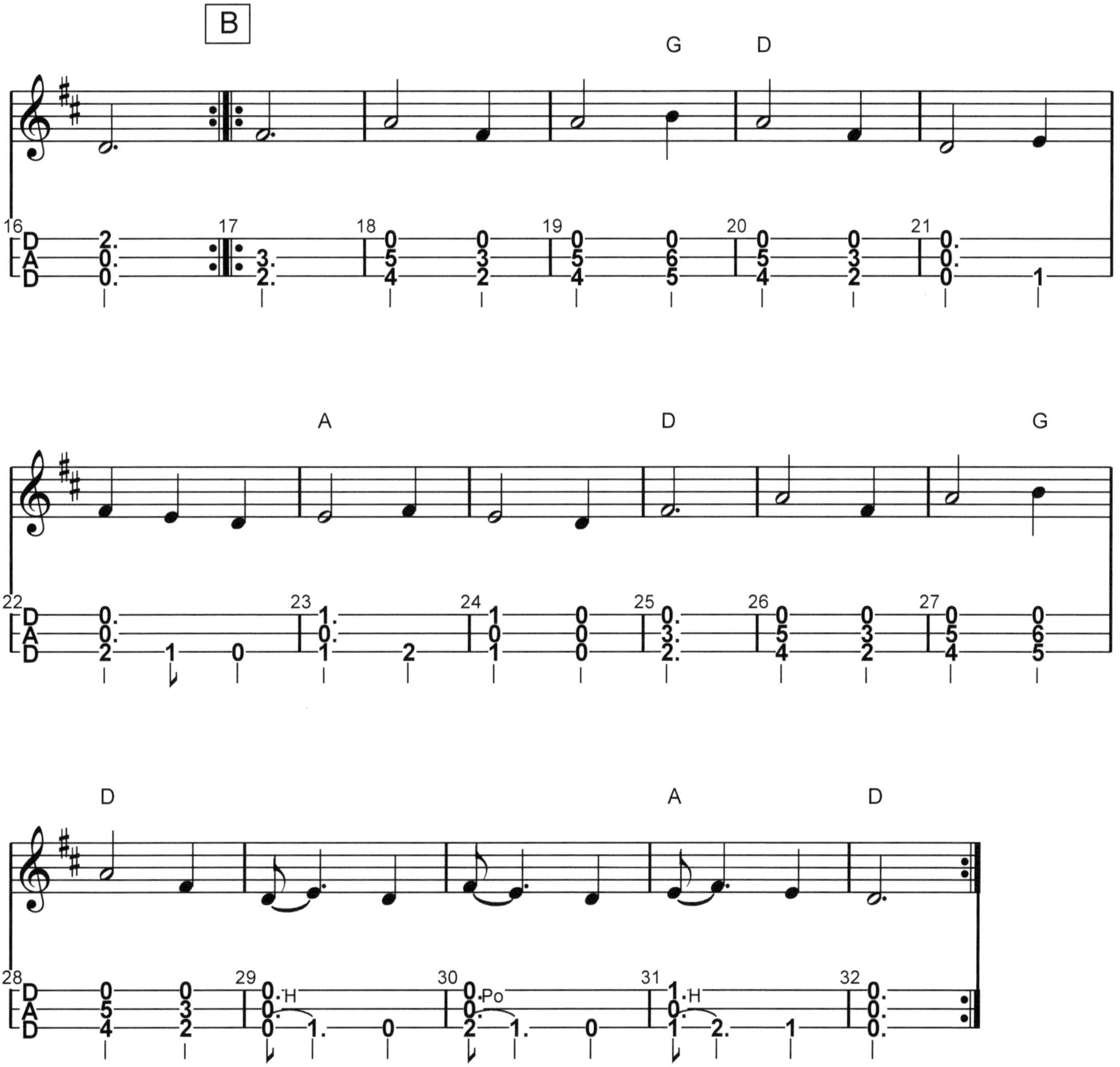
B
G
D
A
D
G
D
A
D
H
Po
H

Expressions

by Tom McConnell
2015

Dulcimer tuning: DAd' (Mixolydian)

15

The Change Will Do Me Good

by Tom McConnell
2015

Dulcimer tuning: DAd' (Mixolydian)

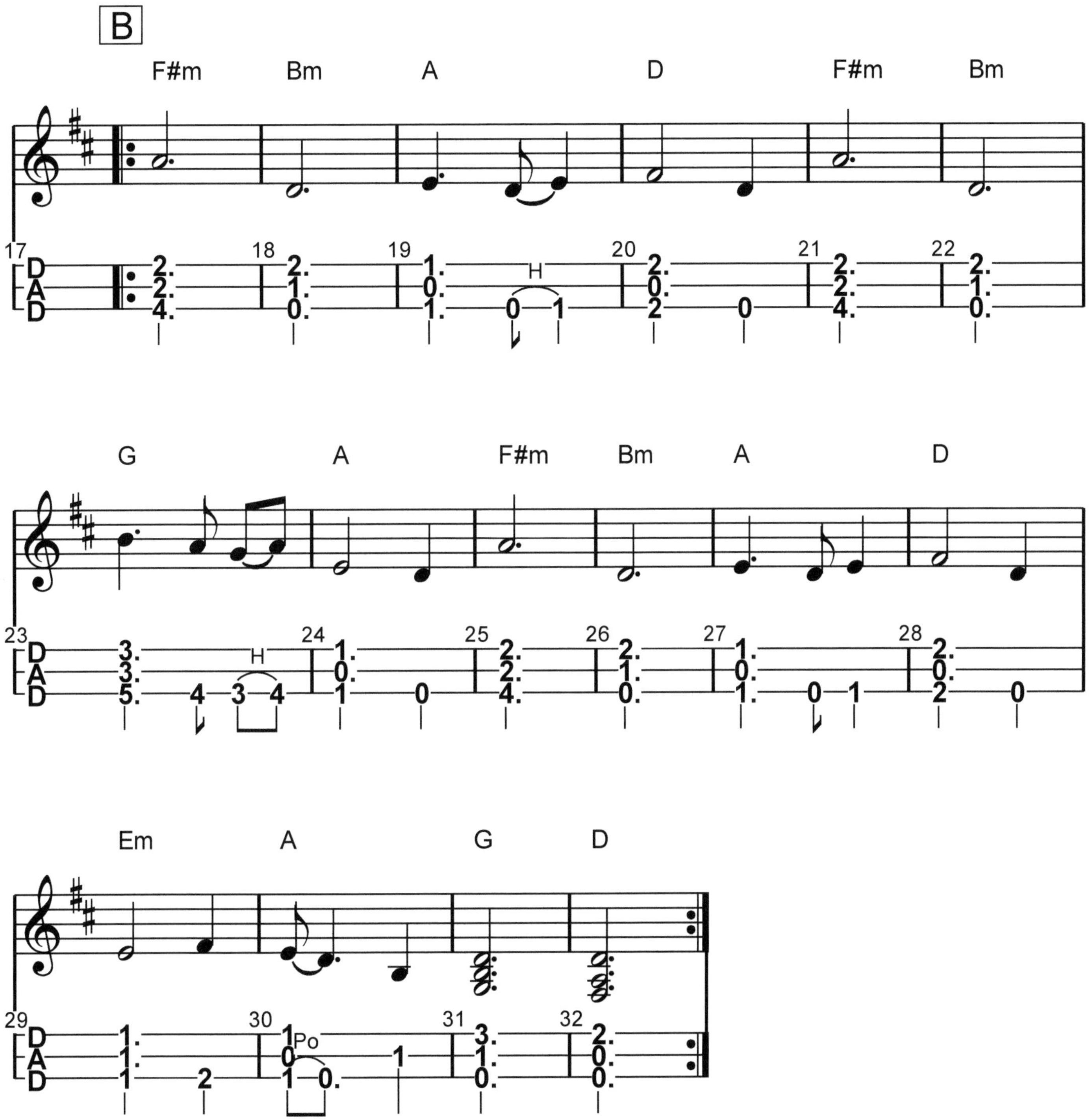
B
F#m
Bm
A
D
F#m
Bm
G
A
F#m
Bm
A
D
Em
A
G
D
H
Po

How I Try

by Tom McConnell
2015

Dulcimer tuning: DAd' (Mixolydian)

B

Wishing for Wings

by Tom McConnell
2015

Dulcimer tuning: DAd' (Mixolydian)

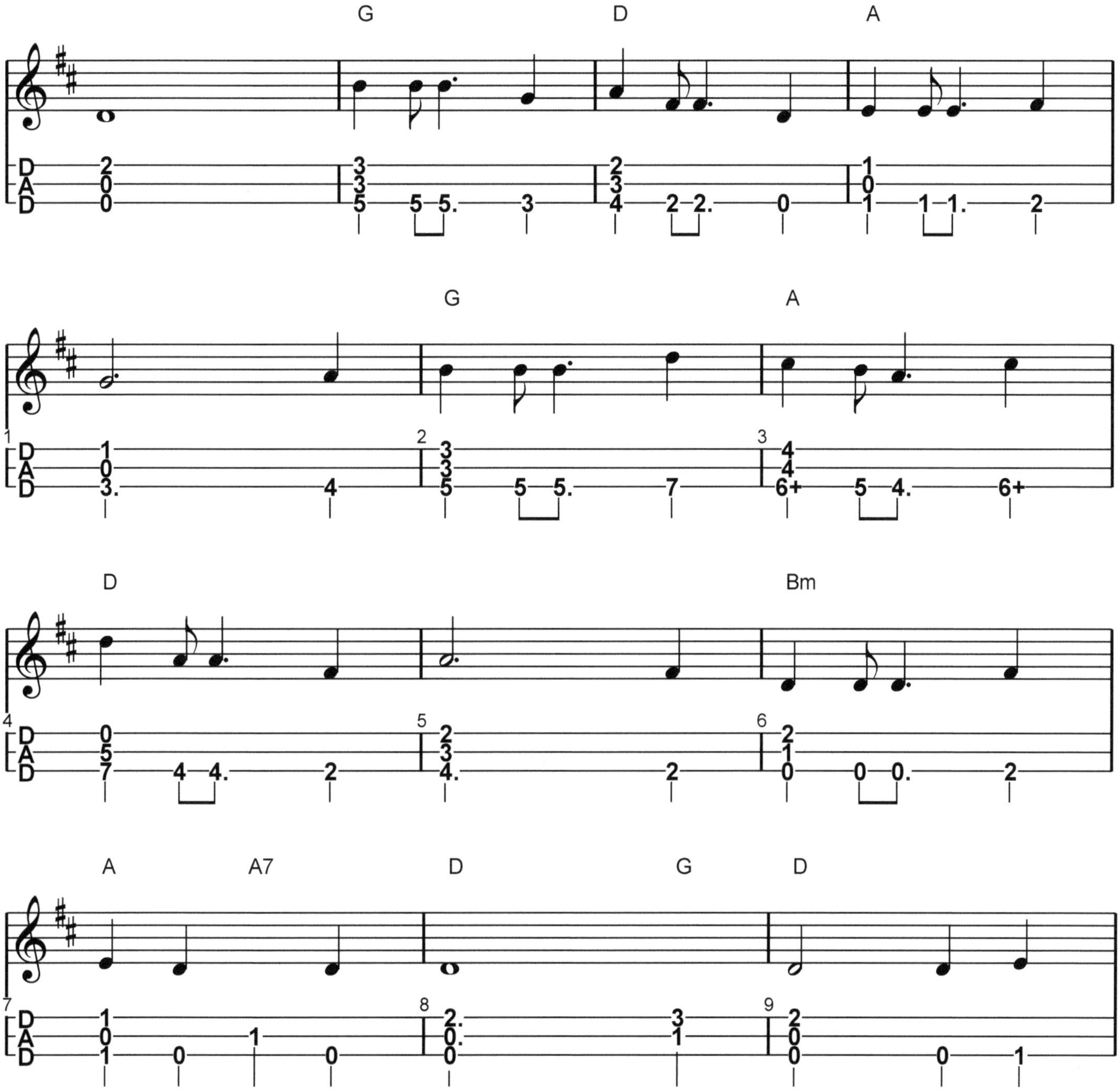
G D A
G A
D Bm
A A7 D G D

Just One More Song
(Michael's Song)

by Tom McConnell
2015

Dulcimer tuning: DAd' (Mixolydian)

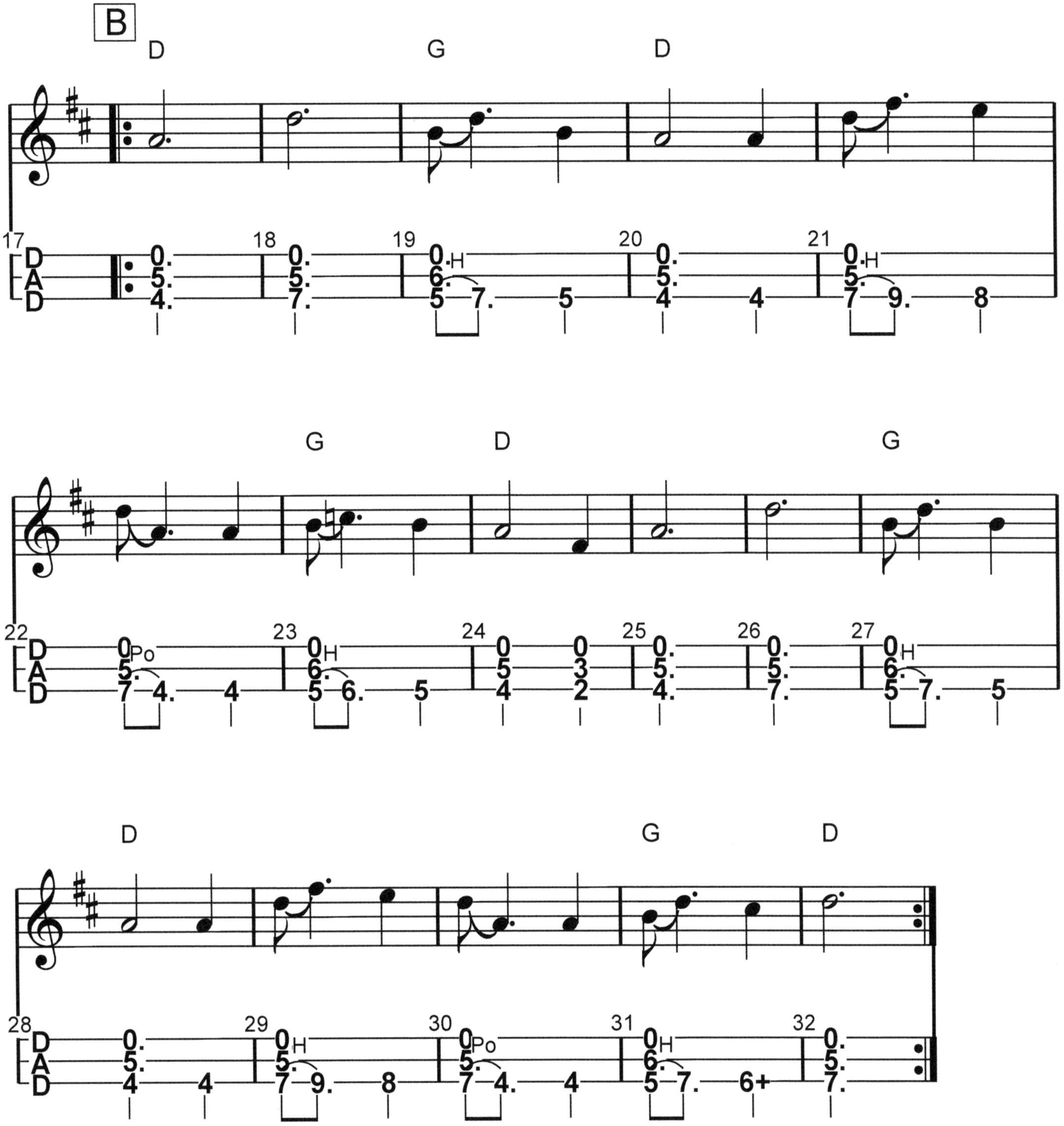
B
D
G
D
G
D
G
D
G
D
D
A
D

Scotty Smiles

by Tom McConnell
2015

Dulcimer tuning: DAd' (Mixolydian)

24

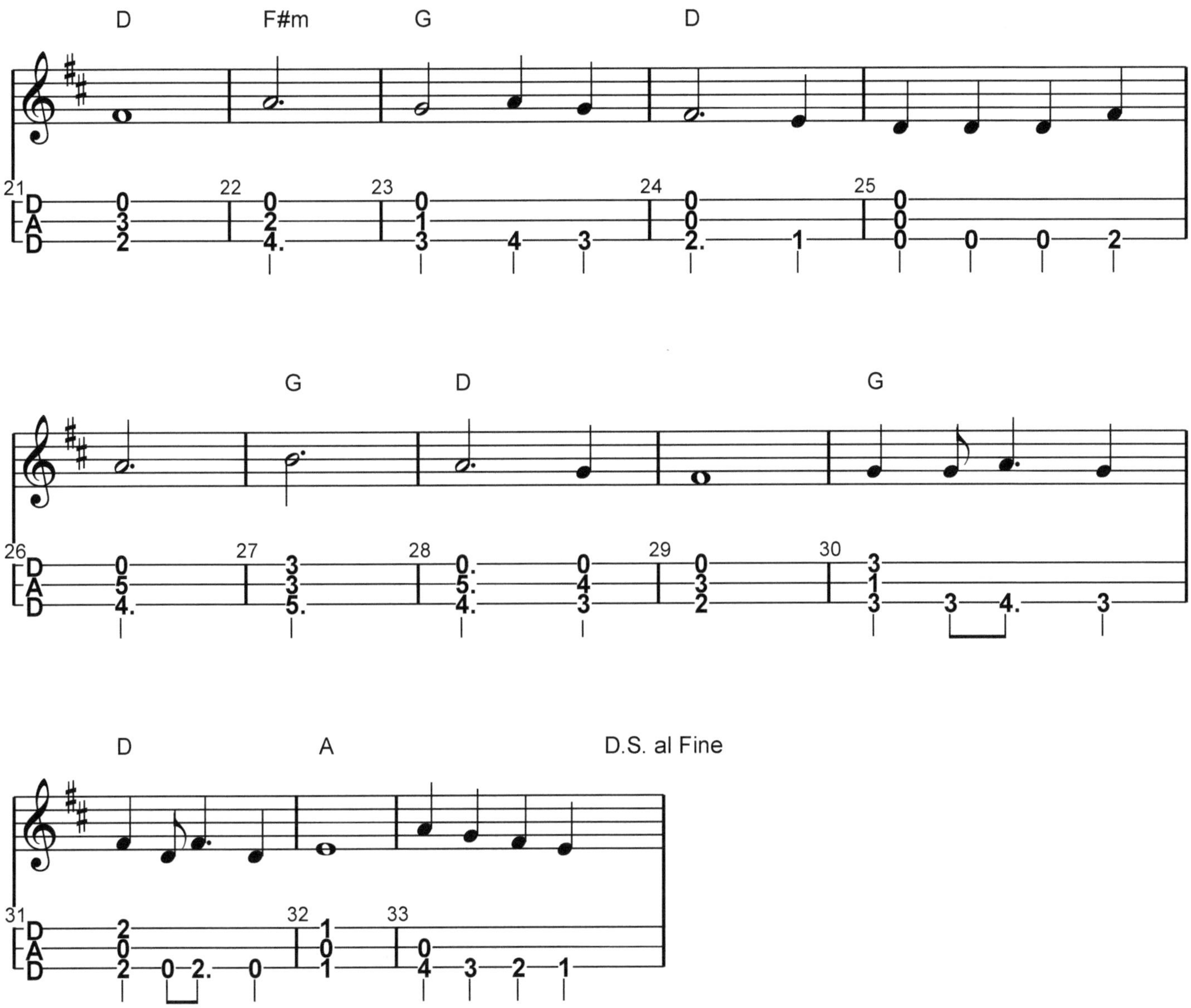
D
F#m
G
D
G
D
G
D
A
D.S. al Fine

The Break of Spring

by Tom McConnell
2015

Dulcimer tuning: DAd' (Mixolydian)

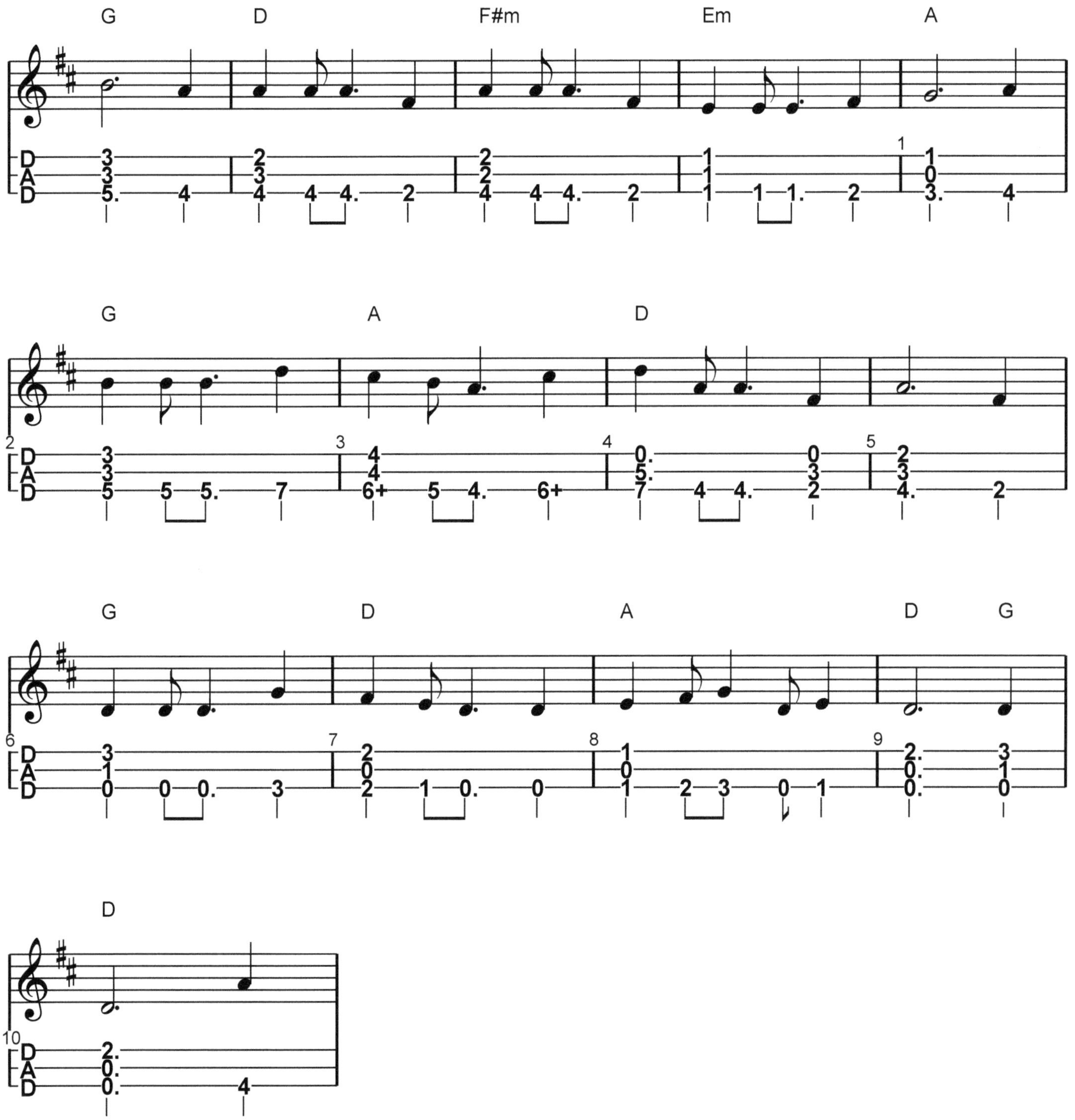
G D F#m Em A
G A D
G D A D G
D

When I Was A Boy

by Tom McConnell
2015

Dulcimer tuning: DAd' (Mixolydian)

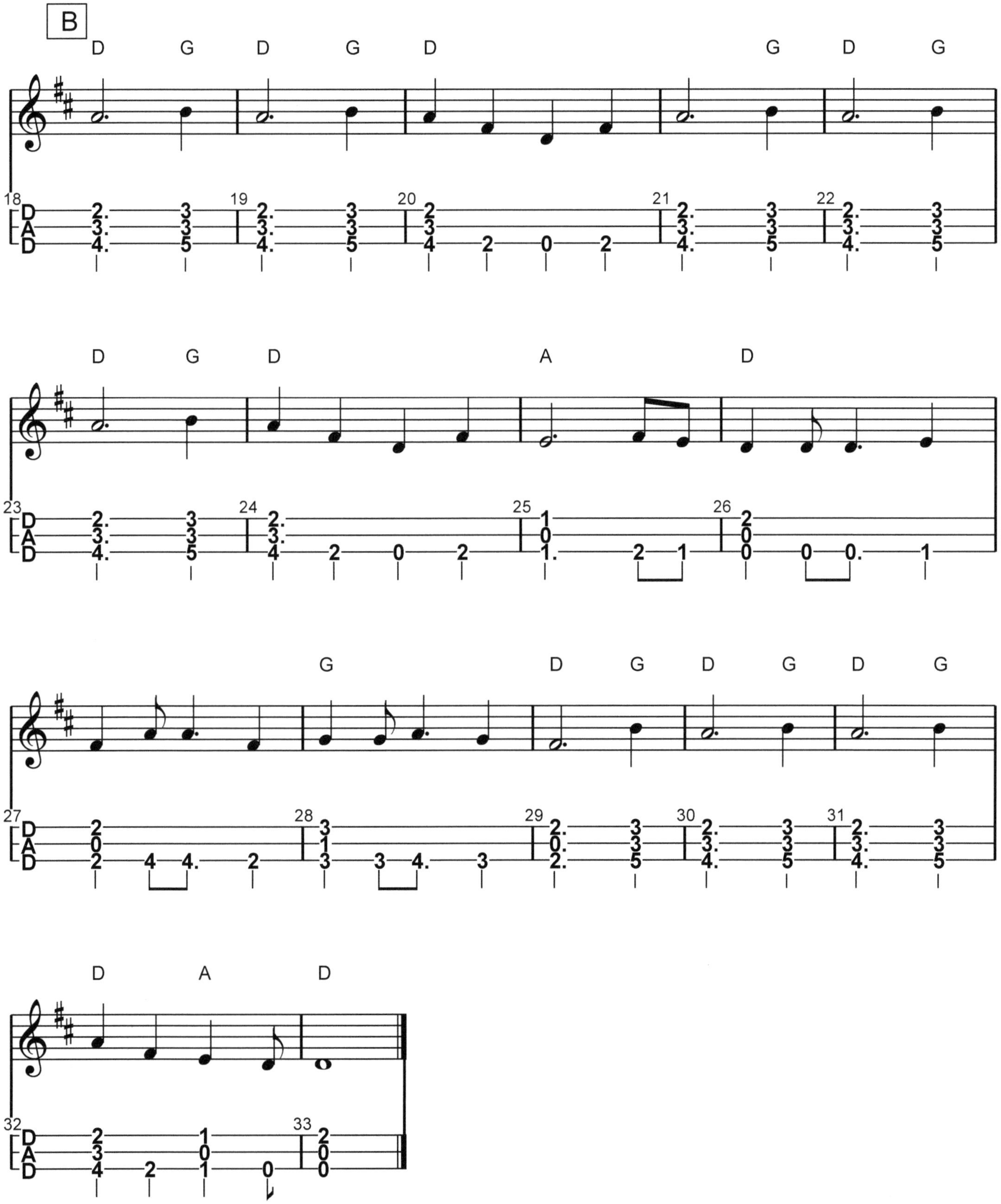
B
D G D G D G D G
D G D A D
G D G D G D G
D A D

After All That We've Been Through

by Tom McConnell
2015

Dulcimer tuning: DAd' (Mixolydian)
Slowly, with feeling. (tempo = 90)

D.S. al coda

INSTRUCTION: Using the Capo, Flat-Picking, and "Chopping"

Hopefully you've noticed that the songs get progressively more difficult as you move through this book. The last three songs in the book are the most challenging, and also present some different twists that need some mention.

Using a Capo
"Letters from Andersonville" and *"Seasons Lost"* are the only songs in the book that use a capo. If you're not familiar with the capo, this small tool lets you shift the key in which you play. This can be helpful when jamming with other musicians who may play familiar songs in different keys, but that's best saved for another book

To use the capo, loosen the screw, press it down just to the LEFT of the fret indicated in the song, press down firmly and tighten up the screw to clamp it in place. Check your tuning when you place the capo – sometimes it needs adjusting. Also listen for a string that is "deadened." This means the capo is not seated firmly across all the strings and needs adjustment.

"Letters from Andersonville" is in the key of E-minor – the capo is placed at the first fret. Minor keys completely change the mood of a song, and I know you'll feel it with this song. The title refers to the infamous Confederate prisoner-of-war camp from the Civil War. The song has a mood of despair that I had not intended when I started composing it, but it seems to fit the title.

Flat-Picking
For *"Seasons Lost,"* place the capo on fret 4. This puts this song into the key of A. Playing this far up the fret gives the dulcimer a different tone, and also increases the volume. I like the sound I get when I capo up to the 4th fret! This song is also the only flat-picked song in the book. Play each note individually... but STILL PLAY CHORDS with your left hand!! Each measure has a chord shape described by the individual notes. In measure one, the notes of the A chord (8-7-6+) are spread out over each beat. This is called an arpeggio... a chord in which each note is played as a sequence of notes. Use this style through most of the measures, but note that there are two "bar shaped" chords in measures 28 and 35. These should be played as a single strum.

"Chopping" chords
"Who's That Knocking on My Door" is a song that looks like easy chords, but the way I play this song adds a level of difficulty that is deceptive. Most of the notes for this song are "chopped" or staccato chords. Listen to the sample on the website. I get the chopping sounds by strumming the entire chord and quickly muting the strings. I do this by lifting my left hand (my fretting hand) just after strumming, but still maintaining contact with the strings. This takes some practice! But it's a useful skill for jamming – you can play chords in a chopped pattern to accent the rhythm of a song while others play the melody. Listen to mandolin players to hear examples.

Letters from Andersonville

by Tom McConnell
2015

Dulcimer tuning: DAd' (Mixolydian)
CAPO 1

Seasons Lost

by Tom McConnell
2015

Dulcimer tuning: DAd' (Mixolydian)
Capo IV

Flatpicked

35

Who's That Knocking on My Door?

by Tom McConnell
2015

Dulcimer tuning: DAd' (Mixolydian)
with a shuffling beat

B
last time
to coda
D Bm A G D G
D Bm A G D A
DS al coda
Coda
Bm A G D
A D
D
A
D

About the Author

Tom McConnell is a native of northern Indiana, and at the time of this publication, he is a science teacher educator at Ball State University. Tom has been playing the dulcimer since 1994 when he bought and built a McSpadden kit he bought from Simple Sounds in Shipshewana, IN. Within minutes of finishing the instrument, he discovered he could find tunes on the fretboard, and the adventure took off!

Almost right away, Tom started "noodling" around and finding new melodies. His early songs for dulcimer and guitar, including *Butterfly Waltz, Just One More Song* and *Back to the Glenns,* were first played for the NE Indiana Folk Music and Instrument Gathering in Shipshewana, and found their way onto Tom's first CD, *Playing from the Heart,* which was released in 2001. The CDs were available through Simple Sounds until the store and the last copies of the CD were destroyed in a fire, and was re-issued in January, 2015.

Not long after, Tom left his teaching job and returned to graduate school. He continued playing, but music took a back seat to school and work. After graduating and eventually ending up at Ball State, he began attending jams and clinics at Folkcraft Instruments, in Woodburn, Indiana. A friendly relationship with the Ash family led to modifications to Tom's dulcimer and a custom Folkcraft baritone that you will hear on some of his newer songs.

Tom now plays with Black Swamp Jam and TRU Ukes, clubs that meet at Folkcraft, and takes in clinics and festival workshops when possible. He's also offering lessons for dulcimer and ukulele, and is working on recordings of a new album of original songs, with a release date expected in early 2015.

Look for more on Tom's musical endeavors at...

http://www.musicbytmcc.com

9 780986 336904